NL

*Psychology book for beginners!
Learn communication,
manipulation & inner strength
Changing consciousness, mindset
& fears with Reframing
More power, success, and energy
through NLP*

General Psychology books
Volume 4

©2020
Max Krone
All rights reserved.
No part of this book may be reproduced in any form without permission of the author.

Table of contents

NEURO-LINGUISTIC PROGRAMMING- MORE SELF-CONFIDENCE, INNER STRENGTH, AND BETTER COMMUNICATION 6

WHAT IS NEURO-LINGUISTIC PROGRAMMING? AN INTERESTING DEFINITION 8
WHAT DO CRITICS SAY ABOUT NEURO-LINGUISTIC PROGRAMMING 13
REPROGRAMMING PEOPLE? 14

THE EMERGENCE OF NEUROLINGUISTIC PROGRAMMING. 16

WHAT CAN NEUROLINGUISTIC PROGRAMMING DO AND WHAT CAN'T? 18

BASIC ASSUMPTIONS OF NEURO-LINGUISTIC PROGRAMMING 21
ANCHORING - THE BASIC TECHNIQUE OF NEURO-LINGUISTIC PROGRAMMING 22
PACING AND LEADING - TWO NLP METHODS 23
OFFICIAL NEURO-LINGUISTIC GUIDE 26

DIFFERENT PERSPECTIVES WHEN CONSIDERING NLP 28

Neuro-linguistic programming equals understanding, speaking, communication 28
Neuro-linguistic programming is about language 29
Neuro-linguistic programming – mental performance 30
Neuro-linguistic programming is the study of subjective experiences 31

AREAS FOR THE USE OF NEURO-LINGUISTIC PROGRAMMING 32

Business life and economy 33
Discover your potential 34
Use of NLP in counseling and psychotherapy 34
Coaching based on NLP 35
In the health sector 36
Creativity 37
Instruction and training 37
Parental education 38

REFRAMING: CLEVERNESS OR DENIAL OF REALITY? 40

Reframing – Reinterpreting with method: one definition 40
Become capable of action again with Reframing 44

NEURO-LINGUISTIC PROGRAMMING AND CHANGING MINDSET 46

THE PERSONAL MINDSET AND ITS EFFECTS 49
BE MORE SUCCESSFUL WITH NEURO-LINGUISTIC
PROGRAMMING AND MINDSET CHANGE 50

DESTRUCTIVE THINKING - PAINTING BLACK IN
THE MOST BEAUTIFUL COLORS 54

5 PHASES OF NLP AND NEURO-LINGUISTIC
PROGRAMMING IN EVERYDAY LIFE 57

USING NEURO-LINGUISTIC PROGRAMMING IN EVERYDAY
LIFE. 60

NEURO-LINGUISTIC PROGRAMMING -
DEVELOPING PERSONALITY AND
COMMUNICATING BETTER 70

Neuro-linguistic programming- more self-confidence, inner strength, and better communication

There are those people who convince with words and body language and who carry away not only one person but a whole mass. Their opinion is accepted and is a supporting pillar of decisions. Everyone is curious about the contribution this person makes. He or she often provides the guidelines and can thus influence situations, events, and decisions. And there are those people who, as a gray mouse, always remain in the background, having self-doubts, doubts about their personality and their way of thinking and acting. Not to stand out or say or do something wrong is their motto.

What ability does the first category of people possess that others lack? Is this an innate ability or have these people worked to be as they are? There is an interesting method by which everyone can develop personally and improve communication. It is neuro-linguistic programming, NLP for short. What is behind it and where is NLP used?

NLP is used in many areas and is applied in therapies, sales talks, leadership, sports, advertising, and other situations. For those who use neuro-linguistic programming, there is the possibility of making their personality more successful and fulfilled.

NLP is a useful tool that can be learned by students up to the boss of a company. The communication model NLP has approached from linguistics, psychology, and hypnosis and is used all over the world for different purposes such as marketing, advertising, entertainment, and the already mentioned Neuro-linguistic programming can also be used for personal development and thus to receive support for a better life.

Accordingly, NLP is important for more self-confidence, self-esteem, self-esteem, and mental strength. And it is exactly these factors that help you to live a satisfied, happy, and better life. Have you ever thought about the barriers that prevent you from living a happy, content life and tried to work on these blockages? With neuro-linguistic programming you can achieve changes.

What is neuro-linguistic programming? An interesting definition

If the term neuro-linguistic programming is broken down into its constituent parts, the result is the following:

Neuro- This refers to the nervous system. It is needed to perceive information from the environment with the sensory organs and then process it. Emotions, behavior, perception, and thinking are dependent on your nervous system.

Linguistics- The term stands for the language. You use it every day to talk to people and have dialogues with yourself. With your language, you express much more than you are aware of. Because you use it to transport the pictorial idea that you have inside you. If you use the phrase: "I let the past be the past", you are alluding to the fact that the past does want to be left behind. For the words are an expression of your inner reality.

Programming-In this context, this means a systematic, goal-oriented change. In the approach of NLP it means nothing else than that you want to change something purposefully. The chosen goal is to use this change as a new basis on which to build and not to have to start all over again.

Meanwhile, neurolinguistic programming has taken on a far-reaching new meaning. Because it stands for the practice of a new, lively life, for new perspectives in life or new learning processes. Since 2013, work has been underway to rename NLP as neuro-linguistic psychology. This would provide an academic claim that has been neglected by the founders until now.

Once you look at those who offer workshops and coaching for neuro-linguistic programming, it becomes clear that this NLP is seen as a big "construction kit with different modules". The modules are models, methods, and strategies to shape your life according to your wishes and to be happy and successful. To achieve this, knowledge about the correct application and mode of operation of the models is important. Because NLP provides you with an exciting starting point for a wide range of possible uses.

From the individual modules, you build your strategies and develop your very own neuro-linguistic programming in a way that suits you and your life best and is most effective. NLP shows the best, most intensive effect in your experience. Because you have many possibilities for applications in practice and during this time you can gain self-experience and go into reflection. And the most beautiful thing about it is that neuro-linguistic programming can be used wherever you communicate with other people or with yourself. Communication is always and everywhere, even if it is not always obvious!

Quote:

"You can't "not" communicate."

Paul Watzlawick

NLP does not only deal with verbal communication and non-verbal signals and a better self-image but even goes so far as to achieve a certain effect with communication by using words, body language, and one's way of thinking. Accordingly, NLP can be used for the following:

- Development of the personality to develop more self-awareness
- Improving and intensifying relations
- Self-awareness - who are you?
- Education - Dealing with the family based on appreciation
- Achieving satisfaction, happiness, and fulfillment
- Effecting changes according to one's wishes and values
- Teambuilding
- Discovering potentials
- Personal development
- Self-efficacy

A little story that might sound familiar to you:

You are dissatisfied with your body, want to change something about it, and register at a gym. The first three months you train intensively and euphorically, change your diet, and suddenly you fall into a deep hole, stop training, and are only frustrated because you haven't kept up with the pace. At this very moment you have lost faith in yourself.

This is where NLP can help you. Because if you believe in yourself and have the right attitude, you will reach every goal that wants to be reached. You only have to deal with your own goals, pave the way, and work on reaching this goal. By using NLP for goal work, you will get a good feeling. Every person has different things to motivate himself with. You can talk about this for example with a good friend or a fitness trainer.

If you want to reach your dream body with defined muscles through intensive training, then you must have an exact idea of what your well-trained body should look like. How much weight do you want to bring on the scales? How visible should the muscles be? By what time do you want to have reached the goal? Set yourself a deadline. If you deal with your wishes and goals and visualize them, you will also hold out and reach your goal. You can be proud of yourself and develop a fantastic feeling.

But how does NLP work in everyday life for mothers, athletes, educators, sales managers, leaders, in advertising and marketing? Isn't the use of the methods manipulation, especially when they are used in political speeches, in advertising, or marketing? Is neuro-linguistic programming the right way to find inner peace within oneself? Is it possible to be as you are and to change the behavior and characteristics that you would like to change?

The statement, which is heard again and again about NLP, is that you should conduct conversations and relationships in a way that corresponds to your values, ideas, and wishes. You should recognize your potentials, unfold, and reach your dreams and goals.

What do critics say about neuro-linguistic programming

In the field of personality development, neurolinguistic programming seems to be the "new" buzzword. However, there are repeated criticisms on this topic that NLP is more pseudo than a science. The reason for this is that, just as with homeopathy, its effectiveness has not been proven in any way. Pseudo-science is compared for example with esoteric techniques and views. Whoever searches the internet for NLP will find an interesting interview with Mara Stix. She is an expert in animal communication and animal kinesiology. Also, there are podcast heroes, bloggers, and various sites that focus on a recipe for success in personal development. Again and again the keyword "neuro-linguistic programming" is used.

It is about self-confident appearance, success in love, and the job. With pseudo-science all problems should be solved permanently and quickly. Through such dossiers NLP advances to an absolute hit. What do the critics say about neuro-linguistic programming?

Reprogramming people?

That sounds like manipulation! If you continue to study the subject, you will find that these methods and techniques are advertised and spread by many well-known personalities. This is very irritating. Because once the form of psychotherapy is disregarded and only attention is paid to human life and communication, it quickly becomes clear how dangerous NLP can be. There are even studies and many documents about it.

Perhaps you've seen Stanley Kubrick's film Clockwork Orange. This film is based on the science fiction novel "Clockwork Orange" by Anthony Burgess. It is about Alex, who is very violent and his youth gang Droogs, who roam the city, robbing, raping, and murdering. Alex has a great preference for the music of Beethoven and glorifies violence. He is eventually arrested and sentenced by the court to 14 years in prison. In prison, he is used as a test subject for the "Ludovico Technique". This technique aims to reprogram the various sensory stimuli to make him a better person. If you enter the search terms neuro-linguistic programming and kinesiology in Google, you will find approximately 146,000 results. There are similarly many hits for the word combination NLP, Hellinger, family constellation. Already when reading the list on the first pages of the search engine it becomes clear that neuro-linguistic programming is often displayed as search results with esoteric procedures.

A further side, which can serve as an important source, is the Web operational readiness level of the "GWUP", where pseudoscientific topics are treated. Here it can be re-read that many Coachings and Workshops offer also various at Esoteric apart from neuro-linguistic programming. Completely typically thereby the NLP mania is in the form of new-age therapies. Because everything can be achieved with it if you only want to, even the physical appearance.

Doesn't it sound somewhat questionable that podcast heroes and bloggers distance themselves from esotericism in their articles?

A long time the explanations about NLP and the offers remind like a combination of helpful visions, misleading ideologies as well as collected calendar sayings and wisdom. Not every star shines brightly on the horizon and what remains is a bad aftertaste. Therefore, it is very important to look carefully that NLP is not used to manipulate other people. It should never stop questioning methods, techniques, views, and concepts. Not only the advocates should be illuminated, but all sides. NLP does not mean to bend other people and oneself to fit into a certain form. Rather it is about becoming yourself, staying yourself, and not letting yourself be manipulated.

The emergence of neurolinguistic programming.

In the early 1970s, psychology student Richard Bandler, Frank Pucelik, and John Grinder, assistant professor of linguistics, developed neuro-linguistic programming at the University of California. The model at that time, however, was greatly expanded over the years.

Grinder and Bandler were interested in advanced learning methods, which they carried out together in a series of seminars. After some time of working together, the two asked themselves why some psychotherapists are successful and others less so. To answer this question, they took a closer look at the success factors of the best US therapists to identify the secret of success. First, the work of Fritz Perls and the successful family therapist Virginia Satir was examined. This was followed by an examination of the success factors of Dr. Milton Erickson. These three personalities distinguished themselves through astonishing treatment successes. The observations were then put together in a simple step-by-step guide. Neuro-linguistic programming referred to these as NLP formats, which can also be used by non-therapists and achieve similar success. They are the basis for the first NLP concepts, which were passed on to a large number of people in later years.

NLP is nothing else than the targeted modeling of methods of outstanding therapists, which have proven to be highly effective in practice. Even though NLP was originally intended for psychotherapy, this method has established itself in many disciplines where people and understanding are the basis. The techniques are used for personal development and to improve communication in the working world, in private life, in sales, in leadership, in advertising and marketing. For many people NLP is something like "psychology for healthy people". Because with it, bad habits can be discarded and changed, relationships can be optimized, smoking can be stopped, weight can be lost, happiness can be achieved and life can be improved.

What can neurolinguistic programming do and what can't?

Neuro-linguistic programming is not considered a form of therapy, even though the basic form is based on the analysis of speech patterns of exceptionally successful and well-known therapists.

NLP is widely used in life counseling, coaching of executives, and as a tool for executive communication, just where it is important to communicate in a goal-oriented way. Therefore, you will find NLP in

- Sales seminars for sales promotion
- Personnel management seminars for better personnel management
- Conflict management seminars
- Social counseling
- Seminars for personal development

The users of NLP are also called Practitioners. They affirm that NLP is not a pure manipulation technique. Rather, they convey the idea that neuro-linguistic programming serves primarily to optimize communication both externally and internally. It is only applied per one's values and morals and must be compatible with the environment. The so-called "Eco-Check" is used as an instrument for this purpose. The changes initiated by neuro-linguistic programming should only go in the desired direction.

"**Future-Pace**" means the correspondence between actions and one's wishes and goals and meanwhile the creation of one's images, i.e. the visualization of wishes and goals. In doing so, influence is specifically exerted on breaking away from bad patterns of thought and behavior and orienting towards positive, desired thoughts and actions.

Neuro-linguistic programming is no substitute for depth psychological therapy, such as the treatment of traumatic experiences. Neither should NLP be used to achieve control over the mind of another person. Rather, NLP serves to recognize and optimize the self-perception and the perception of others, i.e. the image of oneself and the image of others, and to bring it into an efficient and unmistakable form through verbal and non-verbal communication. This also includes the manifestation of the solution and resource-oriented patterns of action and thinking. Linguistic programming is used in

- Business,
- Healthcare,
- Pedagogy
- Jurisdiction

In business alone, NLP offers a fertile and large field for application, since all branches of a business enterprise benefit from it. Thus, neuro-linguistic programming can be the basis for stable communication in successful management.

With NLP, corporate values and goals can be worked out to create a mission statement and unique selling points. At the same time, these become clearer and more prominent. In areas where employees are employed, NLP serves to strengthen the corporate culture. Personnel development and human resources management are largely based on fundamental principles of internal and external communication of the company. The main area of application of NLP is in the sales area. This enables employees to successfully implement management targets set in relation to sales. Employees gain insight and knowledge, which makes sales talks and customer consultations easier.

Customer satisfaction increases and this leads to more contracts being concluded. Therefore, it is not so far-fetched to use NLP for succession planning, company mergers, and similarly important contract conclusions, so that these go smoothly and satisfactorily for all.

Basic assumptions of neuro-linguistic programming

When Bandler and Grinder dealt with the modeling of communication processes of particularly successful personalities, they came across behavior and thought patterns. They deliberately included these patterns in the model of linguistic programming as "presuppositions". These presuppositions are basic axioms on which the human image of NLP is based. Depending on the source, the number of assumptions varies. The following listed assumptions are by no means complete but are only among the ten most common ones that you will be presented with.

- The personal world view, one's map is not the reality or the landscape.
- The positive values are constant. On the other hand, the ways of acting can be doubted.
- All actions are based on a positive intention and have a positive motive for the one who acts.
- The feedback you get on the communication is meaningful.
- There are no deficits or errors in communication. The decisive factor is again the feedback.
- Every behavior is based on a context where it is useful.
- All important resources are already available to bring about change.

- If one action does not work, resort to another.
- The element with the most diverse behavioral possibilities is in control of a constant system.
- If a person can do something, this behavior can be modeled and passed on.

Anchoring - the basic technique of neuro-linguistic programming

Anchoring is the most important technique in the NLP model. It refers to the connection between a specific stimulus and the subsequent unconscious reaction that is desired or undesired. The reaction is based on conditioning. The principle became known through the researcher Iwan Pawlow, who conducted experiments with dogs. The ringing of a bell stimulated the production of saliva in the animals. By ringing the bell he gave the stimulus that when it rang, food was available.

Through neuro-linguistic programming such unwanted anchors can be eliminated and replaced by new, desired ones. This procedure is often used for phobias to release the anchors. Fast Phobia Cure is used to overcoming certain fears and at the same time to overcome all harmful and unwanted behavior such as addiction or weight loss.

The technique also offers another application possibility by setting resource anchors with positive, desired anchors. These so-called resource anchors are linked to a trigger that can be accessed at any time. In the same way, light states of trance can be used on anchors to facilitate the practitioner's work with neuro-linguistic programming.

Pacing and Leading - two NLP methods

There are several ways in neurolinguistic programming to connect with another person. This connection, also known as rapport or pacing, is a communication wire. "Pacing" is a kind of mirror technique, whereby the interlocutor, like a coach, adjusts to the other person and imitates the style of communication. A mirror image is created in which the coach shows through subtle feedback that he is on the same wavelength as the interlocutor.

If a relationship of trust can be established in this way, the coach switches over to **"leading"**. In doing so, he or she takes the lead in the conversation. This can also be used to manipulate the other person to influence certain actions. However, this is not what should be the basis for neuro-linguistic programming. Leading should rather be used to bring about alternative perspectives on the other person's problems and to work out possible solutions.

Formats in neurolinguistic programming are methods or techniques. There is no underlying theorem based on scientific theory. Neither are there any established methods. Neuro-linguistic programming is rather a hodgepodge of different approaches that are possible to bring about a change in thinking. The communication and intervention possibilities are called "**formats**" and comprise precisely defined sequences of actions and tools that are used for change in a positive direction.

Everybody who uses NLP has his package of tools filled. You can find common and individual formats, but they have one thing in common. They are based on the inner resources that contribute to the solution of a problem of the respective person. They can be used to work through problems from the past. The focus is always on change in a positive sense. Neuro-linguistic programming can be used to reinterpret or reinterpret negative experiences and turn them into positive experiences for future action. In turn, resources are needed so that problems, blockages, disorders, or fears can be overcome.

For this to succeed, clear discussion structures and courses of action are chosen as a basis. The orientation and attitude of the coach must be per humanistic ethics and values. This is because neuro-linguistic programming sometimes involves a light trance or hypnosis. This makes it possible to transport positive impressions into consciousness.

One of the best-known techniques in neuro-linguistic programming is "**reframing**", the reinterpretation, which gives a new meaning to a certain situation. This is achieved by placing it in a new context. Other formats use visualization or autosuggestion. Autosuggestion uses the repetition of affirmations as well as the anchoring of positive ways of thinking. In visualization, thoughts are directed towards the future, creating an image in the mind's eye that represents the state of mind when the goal is reached.

All the formats of neuro-linguistic programming are designed in a way that the consciousness always can separate itself from bad behavior patterns and ways of thinking and to manifest new, positive ones in return. An essential meaning has thereby higher behavioral flexibility since thereby more possibilities for the own behavior are made available. This leads to more freedom and quality of life. Therefore, the moral values of the person and the coach should be in agreement so that the interventions go in the right direction.

Official neuro-linguistic guide

Once you have taken a look at the "official neurolinguistic guide" of the DVNLP, you can read that NLP is based on findings of modern linguistics, systems theory, psychology, and neurophysiology. NLP, therefore, refers to essential processes. These include:

- How a man perceives himself,
- Processes these findings itself,
- Carries out actions on this basis,
- Communicates with others,
- Learns and changes.

Each person has an approach to dealing with his person and certain situations. This also includes dealing with other people, one's job, relationships, and all the things you generally encounter on your path through life. Depending on your perception of yourself and your environment at a certain point, this influences your feelings and the assessment of the situation. So, you may find the same situation as pleasant and pleasant or as stressful and difficult.

Studies and models made for the perception and processing of information are used in NLP to find out which forces, influences, and circumstances control one's own experience and how one's own experiences are generated. On this foundation, numerous models of action methods have been developed in the past decades.

The NLP techniques have a pragmatic orientation and are useful for one's development and for improving communication in the interpersonal sphere. In the field of behavioral and cognitive science, NLP takes the place of studying human subjectivity and using the findings to show a person, a group, or an organization flexible possibilities for goal-oriented changes and solutions. As everywhere in the scientific field, research results in continuous development.

Through neuro-linguistic programming, awareness is raised of various processes that influence one's own experience of situations. This results in even better use of the five senses and one's abilities. This makes it possible to formulate goals more precisely because one's influencing factors are taken into account during the realization. Due to the constant expansion of knowledge over the past years, professional dialogue partners have the opportunity to

- To perfect their understanding of interpersonal communication processes,
- To adapt to the reality of the interlocutor without taking into account the dependence of one's content, methodological orientation,
- To considerably expand your interaction with other people and
- To face the challenges and daily changes with high flexibility

Different perspectives when considering NLP

Anyone interested in neuro-linguistic programming talks to users and searches for information in relevant literature will quickly find that the descriptions are very different and diverse. The different descriptions are based on an approach that covers a wide range. The following perspectives are therefore considered in NLP.

Neuro-linguistic programming equals understanding, speaking, communication

That people always communicate is a fundamental principle of NLP. This means not only spoken words. It is also about body language, like facial expressions, gestures, tonality, posture, and many other things. Therefore, the question arises on how people communicate and how they do it. Are you able to express things you want to communicate in a way that the person you are talking to understands? Is there any indication that the person you are talking to has understood you?

How can these clues be used? If you have mastered neuro-linguistic programming, you can draw on a wide range of tools for efficient communication.

Neuro-linguistic programming is about language

The way people speak influences the way they think and react. The experiences you pass on through language requires you to have the ability to compress and represent experiences. You need to express in words how you perceive the environment and thus distort the picture. As a result, valuable information is not conveyed to the interlocutor.

Neuro-linguistic programming provides you with helpful patterns and questioning techniques to shape conversations with other people and yourself according to your wishes. You will gain an understanding of how the use of language influences the way you think and act. Words are like pitfalls and deep pitfalls, as they can subliminally influence premonitions, depending on your choice. It is therefore helpful if you can avoid this. If you are asked not to think about delicious, tasty food, your thoughts will probably only be about the meal. The choice of words achieved exactly the opposite! When communicating, pay attention to assumptions contained in the word and their effect when the word "but" is used. A small example: "I like what you cooked, but...".

The interlocutor often tends to forget the first part of the sentence because he expects the following words to be a negative statement. Take a closer look at advertising in the media and speeches by politicians. They specifically use a certain language with which messages are conveyed and anchored in the minds of the listeners. The inflowing influences that penetrate the consciousness can be recognized with NLP. This results in a kind of protection for their mind.

Neuro-linguistic programming – mental performance

Neuro-linguistic programming provides a precise description of the mental processes and perception from which people build their reality. What is the basis of this knowledge you have? How is it that you feel fear in certain situations and are happy in other situations? Why do you like things and others not? Why is it that you learn one thing easily and have difficulties with other things?

Neuro-linguistic programming provides you with an instruction manual, with models of which your brain can encode experiences. If you understand the basis on which your brain makes different decisions, it is much easier to bring about change, learn new things, and communicate correctly.

Neuro-linguistic programming is the study of subjective experiences

Each person perceives the world in his way, reacts to it, and learns from the experiences. With NLP there is the right tool to tune in and adjust to cultural, subcultural, and individual idiosyncrasies. Neuro-linguistic programming explores what you create for subjective experiences from the interaction of perception filters, feelings, thoughts, and actions. It is very helpful in understanding how a person explains the world and moves in it.

Precisely because neuro-linguistic programming is assuming that everyone does everything differently, no formulas are applied that corresponds to a certain scheme. Instead, through the knowledge of neuro-linguistic programming, you perceive and respect the unique personality of each person and can thus respond to each individual. The differences between individuals are valued. This is an important part of the basic attitude of neurolinguistic programming.

Areas for the use of neuro-linguistic programming

Wherever communication is of great importance for the development of one's potential and efficiency, neuro-linguistic programming can be used to initiate an extremely fruitful direction. The more pronounced and efficient communication, development, and effectiveness are, the greater the range of services NLP has in store for you. The application is versatile and can be used in the following areas. These include:

- Psychotherapy
- Pedagogy
- Economy (human resources, management, consulting, sales...)
- Personal development
- Public Health
- Policy
- Sport
- Education
- Justice
- Develop creativity
- Promotion of physical and mental health
- Hobbies

Business life and economy

With the direct use of NLP in business, you can establish a trusting relationship through interpersonal communication, formulate goals precisely and improve the situation in the respective context significantly if the objectives are included. NLP has been established in this form for many years. That is why it is also part of the standard for trainers in a company. Neuro-linguistic programming serves as a supporting skill to see the world with different eyes, to bring about a better interaction with people, to cultivate the relationship with the boss, supervisor, and colleagues and to overcome cultural barriers in a company with multinational employees.

Modern corporate culture also includes training in rhetoric and training in representation skills. Many management consultants and executives fall back on the innovative and creative inspirations of neuro-linguistic programming and use the knowledge for the further development of the company, for the identification of future strategies, team building, and in the area of quality management. Also, NLP is now increasingly used to train employees in the area of sales.

Discover your potential

NLP is used by many people to overcome unwanted limitations and simultaneously is used to find out new ways of behavior and to implement them. In this way bad habits, restrictive ways of thinking, and fears can be overcome. Life gets a new structure that is more energetic. NLP has a wide range of communication choices in its baggage, so you can make better decisions and create the life you want to live in your desires. Ways open up for you that is a good alternative. These were previously beyond your imagination.

Use of NLP in counseling and psychotherapy

Neuro-linguistic programming has become established in many psychotherapists, psychosocial institutions, and counseling centers. The reason for this is that it is based on highly talented, innovative therapists and their support for clients who have found out how to achieve lasting and beneficial change.

The patterns of speech, creative inspiration, and the manner of behavior were never within the inner circle of conscious perception, but outside it. With a little luck, these therapists acquired closer contact with this. Precise analysis brought the patterns of behavior and information to light.

Meanwhile, many people in the world have acquired the skill of neuro-linguistic programming. The different processes have a great variety and sustainability when it comes to personal change. NLP methods are often used to treat phobias and their many different manifestations. This creates access to the client and his individuality. There is always an examination of the inner and outer circumstances. In this way it is possible to integrate the change holistically in the context of values, social bonds, and the different areas of life.

Coaching based on NLP

NLP has also become an important instrument in coaching, especially in industry, business, and administration. Neuro-linguistic programming is used in a consultative form to help individuals, teams, or groups overcome difficulties, plan and implement new ways of working and provide support in developing their abilities. On this basis, goals can be explicitly defined, suitable strategies and the necessary skills developed.

In the health sector

NLP is ideal for physicians, nursing staff, and other persons in the health care system, as health care provision is changing rapidly and not only nursing and medical knowledge is required. Patients increasingly demand from today's health care system that the people working there has a high level of social competence and flexibility. This includes negotiation skills, willingness to solve conflicts, and a certain amount of business management. This is because it is assumed that the healing process is closely linked to the convictions and communication with the patients. The social atmosphere and spatial design of hospitals and doctors' practices have an equally lasting effect on the process of getting well again.

Neuro-linguistic programming shows ways to provide doctors and nurses with the means to build cooperative, harmonious relationships with staff and patients and to communicate in a clear way and concise and contributes to health promotion. In recent years, the focus on neuro-linguistic programming has increased as NLP more often includes aspects of how personal health can be adjusted and maintained, how stress can be minimized, how the body's self-healing powers can be activated, and what ways are there to grasp the connections between manifested assumptions, attitudes, beliefs, and health.

The basis for this is the question: "What is the difference between people who recover from an illness and those who do not overcome an illness? This field of research is constantly evolving.

Creativity

Artists, authors, writers, songwriters, musicians, and singers, who have done NLP training or coaching, think that they have taken valuable things and insights with them. They have come to realize what blocks the creative mind and how it can be fostered. So, there is the Disney strategy, which was developed by Robert Dilts in the USA. This strategy presents strong aspects of how to release blockage and how to stimulate and release creativity again.

Instruction and training

NLP also aims to consciously develop an understanding of how a person learns and integrates new knowledge into the already existing knowledge. This results in interesting strategies for teachers, trainers, and parents to gain methodical and specific access to students and to support them in achieving better performance.

Therefore, the basics of neurolinguistic programming are incorporated into teaching methodology and leadership. For pastors, priests, counselors, educators, and pedagogues who work with groups, NLP is an enrichment in their work.

Parental education

With NLP the communication between parents and children can be promoted productively. By communicating clearly, you offer the child the chance to understand you and to react appropriately to the words spoken. If you tell your child not to do something, the probability that he or she will act unwanted will certainly increase. If the message is pronounced with a commanding tone or threatening tone of voice, the child will become frightened. A good example is a message that is sent with the following statement: "Don't worry! It causes the child to worry even more. But if you tell him to be careful or that everything is fine, you have achieved what you wanted to achieve.

By observing and listening carefully to your child, you will gain an insight into how your child orients itself in its environment and its world. For your child to assert himself in school and the existing educational system, you should show him how the visualization of his state works. In doing so, you will learn to deal with your child's condition yourself, even if it is not yet the way you want it to be. Parents are only human!

Parents who are involved in neuro-linguistic programming give their children a good tool for successful, clear communication and simultaneously the right tools for learning and developing their self-esteem.

Reframing: Cleverness or denial of reality?

Sometimes it is very helpful to look at situations, events, and things from a different perspective. It is especially useful when you have just reached the point where nothing is moving anymore. Psychology offers you reframing as a method for this, which is also used in neuro-linguistic programming. Because NLP also uses the effect of reinterpretation to see things in a new context and thus come a little closer to the solution. Reframing is not only ideal when crises arise in life, but also helps in daily life to achieve a more positive attitude and more satisfaction. But what is reframing and how does it work?

Reframing – Reinterpreting with method: one definition

Frame refers to a procedure used in neurolinguistic programming and family therapy. Reframing is something every person does every day and often completely unconsciously. Thereby events are interpreted within the framework of certain expectations, thought patterns, and assignments. They thus give them a certain framework, which, depending on the perception of the day, presents itself differently. This results in a positive or negative reinterpretation.

In the long run, it is very difficult to live with negative interpretations because they mean an inadmissible restriction to partial aspects. Every person who wants to change something resorts to positive thinking to do something about it. Theoretically, this is nothing other than reframing or neuro-linguistic programming, since things are no longer viewed under negative but under positive signs. But how does Reframing work? It is very easy. You give a new, different meaning or sense to an event or a certain situation by relating it to another context. To illustrate this, here are some examples.

How you look at a situation depends on several things. These include the shape of the day and your basic attitude, whether it is positive or rather negative. Both are reflected in reframing. Think about a half-filled glass of water. You know the famous question: "Is it half full or half empty?" If you look at it objectively, you always get the same picture. However, many facets are based on perspective. The following are very practical examples from professional life:

- If your boss is yelling at you from the side as soon as you arrive at the office in the morning, he may have gotten up on the wrong side of the bed first, or he may have fought with his wife or children early in the morning.

- The fact that you didn't get the dream job after all has a good side because you don't have to leave your familiar, loving environment and move.

These examples inevitably raise the question of whether reframing is perhaps a denial of reality or a creative way of coping. Critics call it self-deception, as this technique is used to make negative things nice. However, those who only talk about the negative things up beautifully have not understood the meaning of reframing and neuro-linguistic programming. After all, it is not about suppressing unpleasant things and feelings and quickly putting on rose-colored glasses again and creating a feel-good zone. Just like positive sensations and ways of thinking, negative and unpleasant situations, thoughts, and feelings such as anger or grief have a right to exist.

Reframing is all about finding the right mediocrity. For example, Intveen says:

Everybody knows that bad news affects the way you think and that it is hard to get a clear thought. In the vernacular this is called a blow to the forehead. The brain is flooded with stress hormones at this moment. They make thinking suddenly become difficult.

Many people tend to pay too much attention to this deficit. Only the obvious is seen, namely the things that immediately come to the fore. Beautiful things and small successes that lie in the past are no longer present and have disappeared in a gray area.

Once again, the event of the dream job cancellation is taken up: self-deception would be if you told yourself that you did not want the job at all. In doing so, you simply put aside your bad feelings. Meanwhile, you prevent yourself from reflecting critically on yourself. There must have been objective reasons why you did not get this dream job.

If reframing is used, the experienced situation gets completely new facets. To succeed, the question begins with "What for?". But often the question is asked first: "Why me?"

Intveen has a good explanation of why the question of "why" is not helpful at all. She assumes that the gaze is stuck on the problem. One's thoughts move in a hamster wheel and can neither stop it nor get out of it. There are no satisfactory answers. You might get them if you ask the company. But you cannot be sure that you will get an honest answer.

If, on the other hand, you start the question with "what for", you start looking for the context and a new possible framework.

- What's the point of getting a refusal?
- What is the point of staying in the company and the familiar surroundings?
- What can the experience gained be used for?

Become capable of action again with Reframing

You have certainly heard many times from others the sentence: "Who knows what this is good for!" This small sentence does not mean resignation at all but shows that this person looks at situations and events with a good measure of composure. Setbacks are part of life. An important factor for success is the handling of crises. This is why learning resilience is so important. And the sooner you start and the better you can do it, the easier it will be for you to deal with future problems.

An important aspect of this is the development of better self-esteem and that you can tackle your goals. Reframing can be used to bring things back into the right shape. **Karin Intveen** believes that reframing expands your thinking, takes you out of uncertainty and anger, and helps you to regain some maneuverability.

The question "What is it good for?" can be used anytime and anywhere. Given the many crises at the moment, this question may sound rather questionable. However, the background is more practical. Surely, for example, a loss of a job and the lack of income can be seen like this but it could also be viewed from a different angle:

- Now is the chance to find a new job with better earnings, nice colleagues, and more flexible working hours.
- Now the opportunity is there to reposition yourself and do something different, to realize yourself.
- Now I have the time to take care of other people and things that are close to my heart.

Reframing can bring up questions that have funny and ironic answers and make you laugh when they are looked at more closely. Even if it is perhaps a kind of gallows humor, these will spur you on to new ideas. What is important is that you use the method to be mentally always on the move.

Reframing sets no limits to your thoughts and ideas. So, you can mix situations or problems with colors, humor, questions, and even music. Once again the rumbling bass in the early morning in mind, you can imagine him in your imagination as angry Donald Duck, who grumbles incomprehensibly and turns red with rage. Reframing is a great benefit, as it allows you to relax not only your head but also your entire body. It is much more pleasant to live and more goal-oriented in terms of problem-solving. If your thoughts always circle the problem in a cramped and stubborn way, no new perspectives will arise and no solutions will be found.

Neuro-linguistic programming and changing mindset

You are probably familiar with the unpleasant feeling that creeps up on you in certain situations and causes you to break out in a cold sweat because you do not feel up to it. Then perhaps now is the right time to think about reprogramming your thoughts and manifesting a new mindset.

Your mindset is based on formative experiences and memories that are no longer present but slumbering in your subconscious. You can still have such a great effect today, which sometimes gets in the way and prevent the further development of existing potential. With neuro-linguistic programming and the right mindset you can overcome such obstacles and finally be successful. But what is Mindset anyway? This English word can be translated and interpreted in many ways. A general interpretation can be as follows:

- Philosophy of life
- Way of thinking
- Setting
- Attitude
- Orientation
- Attitudes
- Worldview
- Mentality

Your attitude and way of thinking on a certain topic have a great influence on how you feel and act. Mutually, there is a connection that is shaped by the experiences you have made. It is not only the negative attitudes and thoughts that prevent you from being successful because you do not trust yourself to do certain things. It is also positive experiences that you have made in certain areas that strengthen and encourage you.

Maybe you had to give a presentation in your school days and got stuck in the middle of it. That caused a lot of resentment in the school class. This experience still accompanies you today and takes over your entire way of thinking, for example when you have to give a presentation. You have manifested in your thoughts the belief that you are a bad speaker and avoid speaking and taking a stand on a particular topic in any situation.

If you had had different experiences at that time, it would not be difficult for you to speak in front of others today. Because of the positive experience of the past has made you a self-confident person. You know your abilities and can use them purposefully. Your mindset is like a filter that determines your environment in the background according to your imprint and meanwhile explores your possibilities. Now the question arises, however, whether negative experiences inevitably lead to the fact that you are a bad speaker according to the above example. Or is your attitude based on a situation you have experienced and you no longer want to expose yourself to this negative experience? In your environment some people seemingly master every situation in life with flying colors and who know no fears. You have already been born with incredible talent. Stop! Maybe some people have this ability a little bit in their genes. Maybe you have acquired this ability first and have completed appropriate training.

In studies, psychologist **Carol Dweck**, who mainly deals with motivation, has come up with an interesting theory. According to this assumption there are two mindset forms. On the one hand, there is the Fixed Mindset, the inflexible, rigid, and on the other hand there is the Growth Mindset, the dynamic and growth-oriented.

Those who belong to the Fixed Mindset category often believe that certain abilities are innate and are seen as a talent. If they fail at a task, this is attributed to a lack of aptitude and talent. People who belong to the Growth Mindset category, on the other hand, have the firm conviction that with the right commitment, anything can succeed. Such a mindset not only reduces stress but also leads to more success.

The personal mindset and its effects

Studies by Dweck have revealed that people who were often praised for their intelligence in childhood have developed a rigid mindset, unlike those who were praised for their efforts. The tendency here is towards a dynamic mindset. But what do people with a rigid mindset and a dynamic mindset look like?

People with a Fixed Mindset
- Avoid challenges when they could lead to defeat.
- They are not good at dealing with defeat and try to hide it.
- They have the conviction that they have a talent in only one area.
- Negative beliefs are repeated again and again.

People with a Growth Mindset
- are eager to learn, curious, and never miss a chance to learn something new and expand their knowledge.
- Have the knowledge that they have to make an effort to reach a certain goal.
- See mistakes and defeats as great opportunities and learn from them.
- They know their weaknesses and work on them.
- Challenges are the elixir of life for them.

- They have an open attitude towards new ways and experiences that they encounter on their path of life.

Accordingly, people with a Growth Mindset spend more energy to achieve something in life and to bring about change, even if defeat is often inevitable. Such people do not have the belief that they are highly gifted. But they do believe that everyone can bring out the best in themselves if they just work at it.

Be more successful with neuro-linguistic programming and mindset change

The word success is a heavyweight and always weighs on one's shoulders. Have you ever asked yourself in your life what you want to be successful in?

- Maybe on the job?
- In love?
- At sports?

People who want to be successful and are successful have the knowledge that they need to develop and be open to new experiences. And they even enjoy doing that. You can take such people as role models to find a new mindset and use neuro-linguistic programming to positively change and strengthen your way of thinking and attitude.

There are enough people who have had similar experiences and have discarded old thought patterns. They have realized that standing still means certain death and has finally begun to move forward! Of course, certain traits, such as sensitivity to wrong decisions, can be an obstacle and help you develop a certain way of thinking. But according to **Dweck** you can influence the way of thinking by interactions. By counteracting your negative thoughts and fears, you reduce the pressure, learn new things about yourself, discover previously unknown, hidden abilities, maintain a better relationship with yourself and your environment, and can communicate, openly, and honestly.

Changing the mindset is a process that can be achieved with the following suggestions:

- Open yourself to new things, take on challenges, and practice dealing with defeat. Nothing is eaten as hot as it is cooked. People make mistakes and setbacks are just as much a part of life. If you want to achieve something in life, you have to become active. This includes not only the willingness to learn something new but also to take new, perhaps unknown paths. If something does not work in the chosen way, there are always one or more other options.

- Be patient and stop limiting yourself through negative beliefs. Strike phrases like "I can't do this" from your vocabulary. Maybe you are only missing one building block of knowledge about how to accomplish the task. You can acquire this missing piece. Cheer yourself on and use the many possibilities, such as neuro-linguistic programming and reframing. Because with the right attitude, more self-confidence, self-assurance, and self-love, the chances of reaching new shores are excellent.

- Take on the challenges that are presented to you. No matter whether it's the grumbling boss or a difficult task. Take up the challenge and make the best of it. Don't let your negative thoughts influence you, but paint beautiful, funny pictures in your thoughts. The stress level will decrease and you will feel less fear towards a grumbling boss or a difficult task.

- Do not make too perfectionist demands on yourself, even if improvements are always possible. The Pareto principle offers a good orientation. So train your skills and expand your knowledge.

- Learn the right way to deal with defeats and setbacks because they are part of life.

For example, neuro-linguistic programming helps you to communicate better and to present your wishes and ideas in a way that is understandable to others. Setbacks and defeats often result from choosing the wrong words and thus creating a false image.

Destructive thinking - painting black in the most beautiful colors

You are certainly also familiar with these painful thoughts that arise in different life situations, although you have vowed not to give them any more space. You have firmly resolved to put it behind you and to have beautiful thoughts instead. But again and again negative ways of thinking find a back door or a loophole.

Another person pronounces a certain sentence, a special song is played on the radio and a situation arises that turns on the inner film projector. Unfortunately the wrong film is inserted. Negative feelings like disappointment, sadness, fear, anger, and resentment arise. Now would be the perfect time to stop the film and turn off the projector. Unfortunately, this doesn't always work that easily and the negative cinema in your head sucks up all your thoughts.

A cycle is created, an undertow, which pulls you down with it or makes you fly higher because negative as well as positive thoughts create this effect. You must learn to promote the positive circulation of thoughts and the pleasant feelings that go with it. This is not difficult at all since an increase is always possible. But what about the negative head cinema?

The real challenge is that you leave the cinema with negative emotions in time. Many people, however, stay and take a closer look at the negative thoughts the film generates in the head cinema, and fall into the belief that this situation must be dealt with at all costs and helps to be prepared for such a situation next time. In the same way, these negative thoughts are used to vent one's inner rage.

However, this is a completely wrong approach because it only pulls you deeper into the suction. You enter into an endless loop, which means that you reproduce the negative sensations in similar events. There will always be such events or situations in your life so that you can hardly step out of this spiral. It's perfectly all right if you want to work through a particular situation. However, this should be done based on a clear concept in which goals are clearly defined. Otherwise, you will only vent your anger and will feel the payback. Be prepared for the next time a similar situation occurs. Is that what you want? When you think about it, it quickly becomes apparent that you cannot prepare yourself because it usually turns out differently than you imagined in your thoughts. On the destructive level, avoidance works if you avoid thinking about it.

If you conclude that a negative film is running in your mind, you should leave the cinema immediately. Unfortunately, this is exactly what most people find difficult. Imagine that you could influence which film is playing and decide that only positive films are shown.

There would be silence and you could finally enjoy your life in the present. There is an ingenious method for this, which is equipped with a long-term effect. It is very easy to use. All you have to do is to make the negative film unrecognizable and destroy it so that the destructive form cannot be played back. This does not erase the negative situation, but it does not trigger any more negative feelings. You succeed in looking at the situation neutrally or with a smile.

To help you achieve this, neurolinguistic programming offers you a highly effective method that is very promising and works very well. It not only reprogrammed negative thoughts into a positive way of thinking but also dissolves misguided, blocking beliefs and replaces them with new, positive ones. Your beliefs also influence your self-image, your perception of others, and the communication with yourself and others. NLP, therefore, helps you to live a more fulfilled and happy life and simultaneously releases enormous energies that make you successful. Finally, it is time to stop wasting energy on things that do not get you anywhere. Your focus is on the things that will help you to happiness and success. Inner harmony is established and you can go through life with ease.

5 phases of NLP and neuro-linguistic programming in everyday life

As you already know, NLP can be used in many areas. You encounter NLP every day publicly media, in business, in private life, in your job, in politics, and in many other areas where others want to influence you. For this purpose, methods are used that are goal- and success-oriented. After all, it is all about modeling behavior that can simultaneously influence your way of thinking.

A small example: Imagine a genius speaker like Barack Obama or a genius like Steve Jobs and a person who does the same job, but has only average command of the task and performs it accordingly. In neuro-linguistic programming, the question is now raised as to what special characteristics distinguish the approach of the genius from that of the average person. Conversely, the question is asked why one person is only averagely successful in the same action and why the other person is successful. What is the difference between genius and average actions?

You will get answers to these questions by going through the 5 phases of neurolinguistic programming.

Phase 1: Imitate a brilliant person

Find a brilliant person and get access to yourself. Then imitate the person's behavior without the thought of imitating that person. The behavior is imitated until you master this behavior just as well. This does not work overnight but requires perseverance and discipline.

Phase 2: Analyze and write down the behavior

If you are just as good at everything and master your actions with the same quality as the genius, use your analytical thinking to analyze and classify behavior and write down the knowledge you have gained. Draw up a plan for yourself in which you write down in detail how this genius ticks.

The first two steps lead to you becoming just as competent as the brilliant personality, no matter what skills the latter has.

Phase 3: Keep the knowledge in mind and manifest it

Keep reminding yourself of the insights you have experienced in the first two phases. This process is an important step in neuro-linguistic programming as you convert tactics into knowledge. Use this knowledge to pass it on to other people in a bundled form. With the help of the information, the other person can familiarize himself or herself with a new, changed tactic and understand what is being said.

Phase 4: Review

In phase 4, take a closer look. See if the behavior of this genius personality has been adopted. If necessary, start again with phases 1 and 2. In the repetition lies the success. Nothing happens overnight. Stay on the ball until a change takes place.

Phase 5: The right model

If it is successful, you have bet on the right model. If no change has occurred, start again with phase 1 and keep returning to it until the neuro-linguistic programming bears fruit. These five phases according to Grinder and Wandler require endurance, time, and patience if you want to recreate the 5 phases. But not everyone is willing to do this because no time and energy are required. It should not be forgotten that today NLP is more than ever in the spotlight. These methods have also helped speakers like Anthony Robbins. NLP can be described as a very useful tool to develop your personality.

Using neuro-linguistic programming in everyday life.

Even if there are no scientific studies that prove the effect of NLP, you can achieve a lot with these methods. To achieve this, there are coaching sessions and events that are designed to provide individuals or groups with solution-oriented approaches to individual life situations. The core point is usually the overcoming of certain problems. Coaching is carried out over a longer period to change and improve lifestyles and views in the long term.

But there are also simple skills for everyday life, which you can do yourself without a coach. With the following tips and tricks, you can succeed:

1. Create your state with statement management

Neuro-linguistic programming uses as a basis that you alone are the one who has and should have the choice of which feelings and emotions are predominant in your life. In other words, this means that your feelings should not be controlling you, but that you decide which emotions come to the fore.

In the same way the statement is true that people who control themselves can also control others. For every condition there is a psychology in neuro-linguistic programming.

Just try the following:

Stand firmly with both feet on the ground and stretch your arms in the air your head. Now raise your eyebrows and the corners of your mouth. The next step is to try to be depressed.

Did you manage that? I most certainly did not!

Another exercise:
Sit down on your couch in a slumped posture, let your shoulders hang down, and concurrently arch your back. Look indifferently at the floor, fold your forehead and bring one hand to your forehead. Now try to get out of this posture into a euphoric mood, up to ecstasy.

Did you manage that? Certainly not!

That can't succeed either. Now try to perform the first exercise in reverse. You will be in a good mood, even if something was bothering you before. In the second exercise you will feel depressed, even if you were in a good mood before. It is astonishing how one's posture affects the inside. The same happens with the inner attitude, which influences your posture and is a mirror image. You are the one who always has the decision in your hand.

- If you feel depressed and oppressed inside, you can adopt a taut posture on the outside and thus create a so-called body anchor. In this way you create a positive effect on your inner self.
- You can counteract dejection from within right from the start by paying attention to the posture of your body every day.

2. Counteract the fatigue

Similar to the first point, create your state with neurolinguistic programming. For example, if you are attending an event and you feel fatigued, you can counteract this by simply speaking louder. Adopt a taut posture, breathe consciously, and take in more oxygen. This will help you feel fresher. Use a refreshing, interesting topic of conversation, which can release energy. These actions will transfer to your inner being all by themselves and in a few minutes you will have overcome a touch of tiredness.

3. Pacing: mirror your conversation partner

The topic has already been mentioned and described several times. Pacing is one of the best-known techniques from neurolinguistic programming. You mirror your conversation partner during the common communication.

Pacing can include the following points:

- You adapt your gestures and body movements to those of your conversation partner.
- At the same moment you blink your eyes, like the person you are talking to.
- They take the same leg position as you opposite and cross their legs.
- The voice pitch is adjusted to that of the caller.
- The sitting posture and breathing are adjusted.

Try not to overdo it. Otherwise, you will scare away the person you are talking to. With the right number of mirrors, NLP technology can create a trusting relationship with your conversation partner.

4. Use so-called Power Moves

With these movements you can provide a lot of energy and power from now on. Anthony Robbins is well known for his Power Moves, which he repeatedly performs in his seminars together with the participants. This way he succeeds in charging the venue with an indescribable energy.

These special movements can look as follows:

- Raise your arms in the air.
- Using one arm, strike an energetic hook forward into the air, moving from a bent position to an extended position.
- Extend both arms sideways in a sweeping upward motion.

5. Provide relaxation by breathing deep into the abdomen

As you have already experienced, when pacing, you adapt movements, gestures, and breathing to the conversation partner to build a trusting relationship. What applies to communication with other people also has an important meaning when dealing with yourself. If you are stressed and excited, you can become calmer by controlled abdominal breathing and then come down again.

6. Give your targets a face

The keyword is visualization. This effective technique in neuro-linguistic programming is an extra dose of energy for your motivation. Meanwhile it has even been proven that goals that you have in your head as an image trigger faster actions to reach the visualized goal.

- Imagine the effects of reaching the set goal.
- Produce your film and paint your success in the most beautiful colors.
- Imagine the moving pictures in the most dazzling colors, played on a large screen. Feel free to choose the largest screen imaginable to see all the details. Neuro-linguistic programming often refers to a large mixing console where you sit and edit your film. You zoom in on the images and add

music to them, which you can effectively turn up or down. When zooming, you reduce or remove disturbing factors. In the same way, you can play the film slower or faster.

7. Overcome your inner blocks and make fun of your inner critic

It is not the challenges that block you, but the inner critic who creates barriers that block your path. Your inner voice tells you that you do not have the skills for this or that, that you are making a fool of yourself and that others can do better. If your inner critic wants to block your way once again, you will ridicule the inner voice. You can do this by placing a Mickey Mouse filter on the inner blockages.

You can do this as follows:

- Recall the voice of Donald Duck from an old comic movie. (You also know this when you fast-forward a piece of music or a film, the voices are distorted and remind you of Donald Duck).
- Give the admonishing voice the sound of Donald Duck and ridicule the inner hate voice.
- Afterward, you can get back to your tasks and let the ridiculous voice tell you what it wants to hear. You have more important things to do than listen to that silly talk.

8. Turn your inner voice into an energetic voice
You have put your inner critic in his place. Now listen to the powerful power voice that tells you exactly what you want. To do this, use a powerful, strong voice that tells you that you can achieve anything if you have the will. Do not give up until you have reached the desired goal. Not achieving goals is based on giving up too early. Many people fail because they deviate from the actual goals when difficulties, arise and the feeling arises that the goal is unattainable. This is exactly the point at which you should start again. This is what successful people do. They stay on the ball despite difficulties and problems and keep going. They look for new ways and possibilities to reach the goal and constantly work towards it.

9. Reframing things into a new frame
For you to succeed, your creative thinking is required. This is how you constructively tackle situations, things, and events and redesign them according to your wishes, requirements, and concerns. The focus here is on the way things are viewed. There is nothing in your life that is fantastic or bad. It is up to you what you make of the situations and requirements. Just change your perspective. A situation that burdens you doesn't look so terrible from another perspective because you put it in a different context. To use reframing, you must have the will to touch things and want to shape them according to your laws.

If a situation arises again where negative emotions arise, just ask yourself what this is good for and what you can use these emotions for. Often interesting answers arise from the what for questions and suddenly it becomes clear that the negative situation also brings nice advantages.

- Don't be annoyed when it rains outside, but try to feel the joy of being out in the rain.
- Do not see a job termination as a loss, but as a chance for a new start.
- Turn a sour lemon into delicious, tasty lemonade.
- If your project is not going well at the moment, don't get upset about it, but learn from the experience and start over again in other ways. The experiences will also help you with new projects. Through the knowledge you create a more effective implementation and can better watch out for sources of error.

Besides reframing there is also pre-framing. Here you set the frame before a situation occurs. Preframing is seen by some as much more effective. In business life and companies, pre-framing can be used to work more efficiently because the results are clearly defined in advance.

A practical example of pre-framing at a meeting:
Right at the beginning, the framework and role understanding of the participants are mentally determined very consciously. Thus, each participant knows his or her position, and a pleasant working atmosphere is created. These clearly defined guidelines in advance often have a positive influence on the result.

10. Become a creative visionary with dreams, plans, and critical observations!
The Walt Disney Technique is an interesting NLP trick, with which you unite the dreamer, planner, and critical observer and combine their respective ways of acting. Why many people fail in achieving their goals is based on the fact that they do not create a connection between the dreamer, planner, and critical observer, but are only one of them. But it is only the pairing of the components that ensures the unfolding of the bundled energy.

For example, if you want to write a book that will become a bestseller, go through the following components:

1. Dreamer
Create a picture in your mind of how the book will look when it is finished. What is the topic of the book? How many pages should it contain? What does the cover design look like? Internalize in your dreams that you do not want to write one of many books, but a bestseller!

2. Planner

Now it's time to start planning. You think about the structure of the book and design a table of contents. You start writing, design the cover, and plan the date for publication. Every day you plan and design your book.

3. Critical observer

In neuro-linguistic programming, you are advised to change the location of each of the three components. In this way you create a new framework for each of the states. In the case of a book, you do not necessarily have to change the location, but choose unbiased people who will look at your written work critically and give you honest feedback.

Neuro-linguistic programming - developing personality and communicating better

NLP is a versatile method that is very helpful to you. Advertising and politics show you that it is possible to influence yourself and others in your opinion-making to achieve better results. The different NLP techniques can be used in many ways and lead to better communication of your wishes and goals so that others can understand you correctly. You set frameworks, use a different perspective in negative situations, and realize that negative is not bad but a good chance for change. You create a new basis for your thoughts and actions. This basis is an important foundation for you to be successful, satisfied, and happy.

You develop your personality further, get more self-confidence, self-assurance, and inner strength. You have learned to give your wishes and dreams a face with visualization, you can use reframing to adapt to other people and create a trusting relationship. With neuro-linguistic programming you fight fears and self-doubt that block your progress. You gain strength and enormous energy to finally leave behind everything that is burdensome.

Max Krone
Volume 4 (NLP)

Volume 1 (Positive Psychology)
Volume 2 (Manipulation & body language)
Volume 3 (Psychology for beginners),

and other books by **Max Krone** are now available on **Amazon.**
Just enter **Max Krone** in the **Amazon search bar.**

Imprint

© Max Krone
2020
All rights reserved.
Reprinting, even in extracts, is not permitted
No part of this work may be reproduced, duplicated or distributed in any form without written permission of the author.

Represented by:
MAK DIRECT LLC
2880W OAKLAND PARK BLVD, SUITE 225C
OAKLAND PARK, FL 33311
FLORIDA

All pictures and texts in this book are protected by copyright. Without explicit permission of the publisher, author and copyright holder the rights are protected against duplication and use by third parties.

Disclaimer

The implementation of all information, instructions, and strategies contained in this e-book is at your risk. The author cannot accept liability for any damages of any kind for any legal reason. Liability claims against the author for material or non-material damages caused by the use or non-use of the information or by the use of incorrect and/or incomplete information are excluded theoretically. Any legal and compensation claims are therefore also excluded. This work has been compiled and written down with the greatest care and to the best of our knowledge and belief. However, the author accepts no responsibility for the topicality, completeness, and quality of the information. Printing errors and misinformation cannot be completely excluded. No legal responsibility or liability of any kind can be assumed for incorrect information provided by the author.

Copyright

All contents of this work as well as information, strategies, and tips are protected by copyright. All rights are reserved. Any reprint or reproduction - even in part - in any form such as photocopying or similar processes, saving, processing, copying, and distribution through electronic systems of any kind (in whole or in part) is strictly prohibited without the express written permission of the author. All translation rights reserved. The contents may under no circumstances be published. The author reserves the right to take legal action in case of disregard.

Printed in Great Britain
by Amazon